DOES ANYBODY KNOW WHAT PLANET MY PARENTS ARE FROM?

Books by Kevin Johnson

Early Teen Devotionals

Can I Be a Christian Without Being Weird?

Could Someone Wake Me Up Before I Drool on the Desk?

Does Anybody Know What Planet My Parents Are From?

So Who Says I Have to Act My Age?

Who Should I Listen To?

Why Can't My Life Be a Summer Vacation?

Why Is God Looking for Friends?

Books for Teens

Catch the Wave!

Look Who's Toast Now!

To find out more about Kevin Johnson's books,
visit his Web site: http://www.thewave.org

9709

DOES ANYBODY KNOW WHAT PLANET MY PARENTS ARE FROM?

KEVIN JOHNSON

BETHANY HOUSE PUBLISHERS
MINNEAPOLIS, MINNESOTA 55438

Published by Bethany House Publishers
A Ministry of Bethany Fellowship, Inc.
11300 Hampshire Avenue South
Minneapolis, Minnesota 55438

Printed in the United States of America.

Library of Congress Cataloging-in-Publication Data

Johnson, Kevin (Kevin Walter)
    Does anybody know what planet my parents are from? / Kevin W. Johnson.
        p. cm.
    Summary: A collection of readings on how young Christians can get along with their parents, discussing such topics as obedience, discipline, and respect.
    ISBN 1–55661–415–2
    1. Junior high school students—Prayer-books and devotions—English. 2. Christian life—Juvenile literature.
[1. Parent and child. 2. Christian life. 3. Prayer books and devotions.]
    I. Title.
BV4850.J635   1996
248.8'3—dc20
                                    96–10060
                                       CIP
                                        AC

To Our Parents

Roy and Lois Johnson
Tom and Pat Benson

Residents of Earth
Citizens of Heaven

KEVIN JOHNSON pastored a group of more than 400 sixth–ninth graders at Elmbrook Church in metro Milwaukee. While his training includes an M.Div. from Fuller Theological Seminary and a B.A. in English and Print Journalism from the University of Wisconsin-River Falls, his current interests run along the lines of cycling, guitar, and shortwave radio. His eight-to-five pastime—editing books—takes place at Bethany House Publishers, where he is the senior editor for adult nonfiction. Kevin and his wife, Lyn, live in Minnesota with their three children, Nathaniel, Karin, and Elise.

Contents

Part 1: Livin' in the Nest

Part 2: Findin' Wings

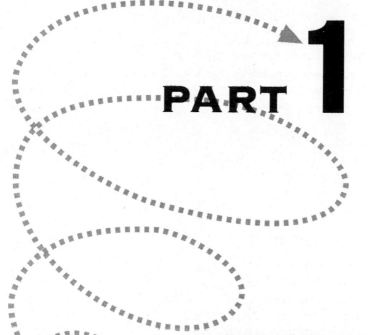

PART 1

LIVIN' IN THE NEST

1

From Mars With Love

Suspicions began to bubble inside your brain the first time you flipped through your parents' high school yearbooks and saw all those pointy heads and spaced-out faces. Your parents, you noticed, weren't the only ones who looked like Martians. So did most of their classmates.

You brace yourself. *My parents were part of a massive alien invasion.*

Your theory explains a lot. You've always wondered why your parents argue about the pros and cons of various warp drives when they watch *Star Trek*, or why they laugh when Mork the dork from Ork says "Nanoo, Nanoo!" on *Mork and Mindy* reruns. More than that, though, your theory answers your truly deep life questions—like why your dad has hair sprouting in his nose. And why your mom constantly fibs about her age and moans about her weight. *If she were back on Mars,* you calculate, *she'd be forty-seven percent younger—and tons lighter!* It even explains why your parents have forced you to gag down broccoli your whole life. *Vegetables are green. Martians are green. They're bonding with their home world.* Only one question still begs for an answer—how your parents could pilot a flying saucer forty million miles but not grasp how to set the clock on the VCR.

And now you've figured out how their scheme slipped by unnoticed. Just yesterday your social studies teacher played a tape of *War of the Worlds*— an ancient radio program people thought was a genuine invasion from outer space. Sure, everyone *says* it was a spoof. *So that's how they landed. That's when they snuck earthside. Everything is starting to make sense. . . .*

Parents are different. They repeat a zillion times facts and stories and advice you've already heard. They fuss about where you go and whether you're making friends with kids who are a "bad influence" on you. Sometimes they stick on strange faces and share that they're "disappointed" in you.

You see things differently.

You're in the middle of a fairly normal conversation with your parents, then *spork broing pfitt*— you're caught in a Martian Moment, that throbbing instant when their utter weirdness convinces you they're from another planet.

But funny thing. If your parents are Martians, what does that make you?

You're a chip off the old planetoid. When your parents blurt, "You'll understand when you have kids," you sometimes don't get what they mean. But plenty of times you do. Hard to admit, but more than once in a while they're right.

There's a lot of them in you and a lot of you in them. You'll probably be a parent someday. And your parents definitely were once kids—although it may have been eons ago in a distant galaxy.

You're not as alien to each other as you might think.

This book will help you figure out where your parents come from. And who to follow when they are— and aren't—around. To use this book have a Bible handy that's easy to read so you can look up the passages where it says ✒ **Read.** (Don't hyperdrive past those!) To learn even more, you can check the Bible verses that show up here and there in parentheses. And pick some Bible passages and stick them in your long-term memory.

It's good you've figured out your parents' secret. You have a big job ahead. Someone has to show them around their new planet.

2

The Big Ditch

"Mom!" Erin howled. "You said I could pick my own clothes!"

"I'm not just going to watch you empty my purse, silly," Erin's mom tried to joke. But Erin didn't think it was funny when her mom tagged along at the mall and trailed her in and out of every shop. Mom couldn't just walk in and whip out the checkbook. She had to help pick everything—down to every last pair of socks. Worse yet, Mom wouldn't dream of leaving Erin's dad and little brother and sister at home. Erin's shopping trip had turned into family night at the mall.

For a while Erin's family didn't notice her walking faster and faster, always at least twenty steps in front of them. No one, that is, until Erin's little brother gave her away. "Why won't she walk with us?" he whined. *Worm.* She'd get him later.

"What's wrong?" her dad bellowed. "Don't you want to be seen with us?"

📝 **Read Proverbs 6:20–23. Why does God stick us in families?**

In the beginning is Dad and Mom. They bring baby home from the hospital, maybe from a foster home. It's cute—love, marriage, baby carriage. But families are more than cute. There's no better place to teach a drooly new human how to grow up.

Deep down inside you probably love your family. Some days you even like them. But growing up means you're in the process of leaving them.

That's where the problem starts. It's part of God's plan for you to have a family to guide you. But it's also part of God's plan for you to grow up, to learn to make your own choices, to live on your own—but most of all, to hang on to Him and follow Him for yourself. Your family has been there to care for you. But you're learning to care for yourself.

You're caught in the middle—sure, you still depend on your family, but your family isn't always around. Already you have to fend for yourself with friends, with strangers, at school, out and about. You know you're not a baby anymore.

But your family isn't always so sure. And unless you want them to treat you like you're still stuck in a stroller, you need to figure out how to get along at home—and on your own.

My son, keep your father's commands and do not forsake your mother's teaching. . . . For these commands are a lamp, this teaching is a light, and the corrections of discipline are the way to life. . . .

PROVERBS 6:20, 23

3

Brussels Sprouts in Squid Sauce

Marcus gags as he spoons a blop of creamed corn onto his plate. "Nate doesn't have to eat this stuff at his house," he moans. Marcus neglects to mention that once he ate brussels sprouts in squid sauce at Nate's house—and liked it.

Dad glares. "You're being rude."

Marcus suddenly bursts. "I always have to do what you say!"

"What's the big deal? You just need to eat what we cook," Dad responds calmly. "Unless, of course, you want to cook instead. Or you could always spend your allowance and call for pizza."

Marcus slumps in his chair and stirs his creamed corn with his fork. *I always have to do what they say.*

☑ **Read Ephesians 6:1–3. What does it mean to "honor your father and mother"?**

Being good to your parents doesn't just mean keeping your culinary critiques to yourself when you think the food is crude—although that's a start. It means even *more* than swallowing hard and suffering through what you know you're supposed to do. Honoring your parents means *respecting them* and *obey-*

ing them willingly—not only because you have to but because you want to.

When Paul wrote this passage to the Ephesians he was repeating one of the Ten Commandments, the laws God had given His followers hundreds of years before. God was never dumb about how hard obeying can be. He didn't even assume that parents are always right or perfectly worthy of respect. After all, God knew that the first parents He created—Adam and Eve—had pushed each other to rebel against Him. And their home life wasn't exactly happy—one of their sons murdered the other (Genesis 3:1–4:16). Still, God said clearly how it's supposed to go: We're to obey our parents.

That's blunt. But God doesn't say that listening to your parents will merely steer you clear of fatty foods and gruesome table manners. As you obey your parents, He promises to guard your life. Parents aren't God, but God's caring hands reach out to you through your parents.

Honoring your parents is right. It's also smart.

Children, obey your parents in the Lord, for this is right. "Honor your father and mother"—which is the first commandment with a promise—"that it may go well with you and that you may enjoy long life on the earth."

EPHESIANS 6:1–3

4

Speak Up or Put Up

"She'd be cute if it weren't for her ears," Allison's dad teased.

Allison's friends laughed. That just egged her dad on. "Did you know that when you call Allison you have to pick which ear you want to talk to? Her ears are so big they're in different area codes."

They all laughed again. Allison didn't. But Dad was on a roll. "We're thinking of taking up windsurfing," he grinned. "We won't need sails."

Allison always hid her ears under her hair. Her ears looked just like her dad's, so she knew he was making fun of himself too. But that didn't make his teasing hurt any less. *Why does he have to joke about my ears?*

Allison faked a smile and got up to refill her soda, then hid in the kitchen popping popcorn for her guests. Finally she told her friends she had homework to do and left to hide in her room. Allison wished her dad would shut up.

Instead *she* did.

> **Read Ephesians 6:4. What can you do when your parents bug you?**

God commands kids—and teens—to obey their parents. But He has an even longer list of commands for parents. It's your parents' job to guide, discipline, and encourage you—to direct you without driving you crazy.

Sooner or later parents goof. They love you but don't know how to show it. Or they know what to do but do it imperfectly. They say things that hurt. They pile on rules and demands but don't raise a finger to help. They snoop too much and listen too little. They cut you down instead of building you up. And so the Bible warns parents not to "exasperate" their kids— to irritate or push them to anger.

It won't help to spit back or to act up or to scream at your parents what God expects of them. But you can *talk* to them. Instead of sassing back or backing off, tell them how you feel and what you need. That isn't an excuse to clobber them. It's a chance to gently persuade them, to talk to them the way you want to be talked to—with respect (1 Timothy 5:1).

Your parents can't change if they don't know what hurts or annoys you. If you don't learn to speak up, your only choice is to put up.

Fathers, do not exasperate your children; instead, bring them up in the training and instruction of the Lord.

EPHESIANS 6:4

5
Butting Heads

Tyler did well at school. He didn't want to.

When all his friends bragged about their bad grades—how low quiz scores could actually go—Tyler began to plot. For as long as he could remember he had studied hard. Now he figured he deserved time off for good behavior. So he decided that at the start of second semester he would slack off. He'd show up for school, but he'd leave his brain at home.

For nine weeks Tyler lounged in total slothdom. Then mid-semester notices went home and his parents found out he was flunking math and social studies.

Pick what Tyler's parents most likely would do: (a) applaud his desire to fail and get him ready for life on the streets by letting him camp in a refrigerator box in the backyard; (b) feed his need to kick back by jetting him to his own lush South Pacific island; or (c) ground him until he's thirty or until his grades improve, whichever comes first.

Easy pick.

☑ **Read Hebrews 12: 7–11. Why do your parents discipline you?**

You know how it goes when you butt heads with your parents. You act or think or feel one way. They make it known they want you to act or think or feel another way. They take it upon themselves to restrain your outsides and reshape your insides.

So does their knack for discipline ooze from an evil plan to ruin your life? Hebrews says it comes from a wish to make you the best you can be. You're hurting yourself, so your parents stop you. You're doing less than your best, so they push you to reach higher. You're doing something wrong, so they help you do what's right. Parents may differ about how and when to step in, but they're programmed at the factory to do discipline.

Their care reflects *God's* care.

Discipline hurts. Training is work. No football player or figure skater enjoys every rule or instruction breathed by a coach. But a coach isn't a coach if he doesn't drill his team. And parents aren't parents if they don't train their kids.

No discipline seems pleasant at the time, but painful. Later on, however, it produces a harvest of righteousness and peace for those who have been trained by it.

HEBREWS 12:11

6

Horsing Around

"But you said I could go," Grant protested.

Grant's mom stood firm. "Grant, if you had finished your chores, you could go. But you didn't. And so you can't."

"I did my chores. I mowed the lawn."

"You mulched two new shrubs because you were in a hurry. Then you ran out of gas and left half of the backyard undone. Remember? And you didn't weed-whack."

"I'll do it later!" Grant pleaded. "I promise."

"You said you would get it done before you left."

"I'll get it done," Grant seethed. "Can't I decide when I'll do it? You always treat me like I'm a little kid."

"I hate to say it, but right now you're acting like one."

☑ **Read Psalm 32:9. When will your parents trust you and treat you like you're grown up?**

Horses are beautiful, but they're no match for your brains. Horses don't read maps. They can't follow directions. When you want a horse to go somewhere unfamiliar you put a bit in its mouth, hop on its back, and *steer*.

Sometimes your parents think they have to steer *you.*

Not long ago you needed your parents to feed, wipe, burp, and bathe you. You learned to walk, but it took a long time before you could cross the street by yourself. You learned to talk, but it was quite a wait before you made much sense.

Changes came gradually. Trust built slowly. The point? You can't fake maturity. You can't pry control away. To get freedom you have to prove yourself.

Your parents may loosen the reins a bit if you conform on the outside—if you do what you're told. But you'll get even more freedom when your parents sense something good going on inside—when you *want* to do what's right. Playing the part of the perfect child isn't enough. Parents want to know you have a brain—good judgment. They need to see you have a pure heart—good character.

Your parents will always think of you as their baby. But if you don't act like one, you up the chance they won't treat you like one.

———————

Do not be like the horse or the mule, which have no understanding but must be controlled by bit and bridle or they will not come to you.

PSALM 32:9

24

7

Real Family

Halfway through their youth group's winter retreat, Chad decided to show Dana how much he liked her. He howled as he roared down the icy sledding run—straight at Dana. He hit. She flew. She body-slammed into the hard ground. What love.

Chad and Chelsea and some other friends carried a sore, dazed Dana back to the chalet, propped her in front of a fireplace, and brought her pizza and soda.

Late that evening around a blazing fire, Dana bragged to the whole group about her shatterproof skull. She said her friends on the retreat—even Chad—were her real family. Her friends were cool and home was horrible. Lots of kids nodded.

As Chelsea listened to other kids tell their stories and hint that *all* parents and brothers and sisters were awful, she felt like jumping up and yelling, "No! My family isn't like that!" Chelsea liked her family. Home was safe. Home was good. But she wondered if anyone would believe her.

✔ **Read Ephesians 4:29–5:2. Can a family ever be friends?**

Some people say that every family is a mess. Here's the truth: Some families get along good most of the time. Many get along well at least some of the time.

You may not live in one of those families. You may live with divorce, violence, or alcohol or drug abuse. Your parents may work too much. You may even have been beaten up or sexually abused—if that's you, find a counselor or pastor or teacher to talk to. You're not alone. And you won't make it alone.

Whatever kind of family you live in you can still control how *you* act. It's easy to be nice to friends (Luke 6:31–35). But you no doubt let yourself do things to your parents and brothers and sisters you would never do to your friends.

It doesn't have to be that way. Paul says that the love and forgiveness God has for you is something you can pass on to the world around you—including your family. You don't have to sass, spew, or slug and turn your family into enemies. As far as it depends on you, you can be a friend (Romans 12:18).

You aren't weird if you get along with your family. You're weird if you don't try.

———————

Be kind and compassionate to one another, forgiving each other, just as in Christ God forgave you. Be imitators of God. . . .

EPHESIANS 4:32–5:1

8
Watch Your Head

Your four-year-old body lies on an emergency-room gurney. You gaze up through a sterile white sheet at the bright lights above you. Through a slit in the sheet, a doctor sews your scalp back together. The doctor asks how you cracked your head open. Technically, *you* didn't. Your six-year-old brother did it for you. He rammed your head into the corner of a chimney.

"What kind of kid would do that?" the doctor squawks. You wonder too. You're no headshrinker, but you think what he did maybe had something to do with what you did to him a month earlier. At your grandparents' farm you swung open an old-fashioned garage door, caught your brother's mouth, and knocked out eight front teeth. Maybe he was mad about that. *I should have said I was sorry. Nah. It was an accident. Did anyone* make *him put his mouth there? Besides, they were baby teeth. They were going to fall out anyway.*

Maybe he was mad about that.

▶ **Read Ephesians 4:26–27. What's the best way to keep your family cool?**

You can't help but get hot living in a family. You live close, share chores, battle over the TV, fight for

27

the phone, hog each other's space, and "borrow" each other's stuff. Living as a family always ignites strong feelings. That's normal.

The real problem is when you overheat.

Ephesians tells how to hose down the flames. "Don't let the sun go down while you're still angry" doesn't mean "Get even before it gets dark" or "Dish it out before dusk." It means this: Talk. Listen. Forgive. Forget. Before you go to bed. While problems are little. Before the flames flare up again the next day.

Don't wait to fix things with your family. And don't forget that a few verses later Paul tells *how* you can get the guts to get over hurt: You can forgive others because God forgave us.

If you gash your hand, you don't wait days to clean it out and stitch it up. Ignore the wound for a while and you'll get a vicious infection. Take a year and it will kill off your arm. Wait a few years longer and it will eat away your head.

———————

"In your anger do not sin": Do not let the sun go down while you are still angry, and do not give the devil a foothold.

EPHESIANS 4:26–27

9

Barf Once
Dine Twice

As Steffi timewarps through the wormhole, her cheeks and the corners of her eyes and mouth all slide toward her ears, peeled back like a rich lady's too-tight facelift. Twenty-some years into the past she jolts to a stop. Suddenly Steffi is watching her mom's life reel by in fast forward.

She sees her mom flirting. She's smoking and acting cool, laughing—drunk.

Steffi waves her hand in the face of her teenage mom. Her mom is startled. Steffi speaks before her mother can. "See, you had your fun!" she accuses. "Now I want mine. You just don't want me to have my turn."

The wormhole begins to unravel, pulling Steffi back to her own time. "You're not seeing all of me," her mom calls out as Steffi blasts away. "You're not seeing what I really thought and felt. You can't see the pain!"

✒ **Read Proverbs 26:11–12. Why do as your parents say— and not as they did?**

When you were little your parents could say, "That's a stove. It's hot. It will burn you." You probably said, "No it's not. No it won't." But you were short enough that they had no problem putting you in your place to protect you.

Guess what? You're not so small anymore. And your parents' ability to keep your hands out of ovens and away from burners is almost gone.

Still, you've mastered the stove lesson. Your parents probably don't have to beat you back to keep you from broiling fingers for breakfast. Why? At some point you decided your parents aren't stupid. Sometimes you didn't know best.

Adults have all done things they regret. What seemed fun at the time—and what might sound fun to you—doesn't look so good to them now. Like a whopper sunburn, the damage didn't show up until later. But they still got burned.

Your parents and other adults want you to learn from your mistakes—and from theirs. To do anything less is to be like a toddler too dumb to stay away from the stove—or like a dog that barfs once and eats twice. He goes back to chomp down what already made him sick, mistaking it for another meal.

As a dog returns to its vomit,
so a fool repeats his folly.

PROVERBS 26:11

30

10

Noseprints on Glass

An hour after your parents were supposed to pick you up at the movie theater you're pressing your nose against a lobby window, staring into the distance, watching for their car. You sit down. You get up to look. You pace. You call again. No answer. You pace some more.

Your friends are long gone. The ushers stare at you half-angry, half-sorry like you're an orphan. Then you start to wonder if you are—if your parents are dead in a car crash somewhere. You push away that thought. *What could they be doing that's more important than picking me up?*

When they finally pull up you dart out, crawl into the car, and slam the door. Your parents gush about the deal they found on a new home entertainment system. They say it will shake walls and melt windows.

At the moment you're not impressed.

☛ **Read Isaiah 49:13–16. Does God ever forget about you?**

Some parents are messed up and hardly know who you are. Others are checked out—they've left, or they spend time on anything but their kids.

Most parents are busy. Someone in your family

has to make money, which means deadlines, trips, overtime, and stress. Besides that, you share your parents' attention with brothers and sisters and other relatives. And parents have to sleep and eat and collapse like everyone else.

And those are the people voted "Most Likely to Be There When You Need Them."

Sometimes the reasons parents are unavailable are understandable. Sometimes they aren't. Either way, you're left feeling lost and alone.

When God's people worried He didn't care about them He reminded them that no mother could fail to care for her child. But even if a mother could neglect her child, God wouldn't forget His people. God told them He had "engraved" them on His hand—a pretty permanent way to write yourself a reminder. He swore that He hadn't, wouldn't, and couldn't forget them.

When you feel your parents aren't there, God is.

Can a mother forget the baby at her breast and have no compassion on the child she has borne? Though she may forget, I will not forget you! See, I have engraved you on the palms of my hands. . . .

Isaiah 49:15–16

32

11

Up on the Rooftop

Julie's parents stood in the driveway studying the snow on their garage roof.

"They're not footprints," her dad said. "It's just the wind."

"It's strange how the wind makes little marks from Julie's window to the edge of the roof closest to the fence," her mom observed, "and knocks the snow off that one spot on the fence—and makes more of the little marks from the fence to the driveway."

"Well, maybe they are footprints. But they're not hers," her dad argued. "I asked her. She said she doesn't sneak out."

"Then how on earth do you think they got there?"

"I don't know."

"So we're not going to do anything about her sneaking out?"

"No."

Read 1 Samuel 2:12–17, 22–25. Who loses when your parents let you get away with anything?

Eli's sons did unbelievable evil—the equivalent of skimming cash from the offering plate and sexually abusing women in the church. They got away with sin at least in part because their father knew what they were doing and refused to correct them. Their father was too foolish to believe what others told him—or at least too slow to act to stop them, even when God warned him (1 Samuel 2:27–36).

Some days you can outwit your parents with half your brain tied behind your back. But taking advantage of their temporary denseness by doing wrong is like jumping at a chance to drink toilet cleaner. If a two-year-old's parents didn't childproof their house—if they didn't lock up poisons and hide medicine out of reach—you wouldn't cheer. You'd feel sad and scared. Freedom from sane boundaries isn't freedom at all.

You're no two-year-old. Ultimately *you* are in charge of yourself and your own well-being. When you choose to do wrong, it hurts your parents. It almost always hurts other people. But it hurts *you* worst of all. If your parents won't stop you, stop yourself. If they won't confront you when you're headed out a window, find someone who will.

Eli and his sons, by the way, didn't live happily ever after. They ignored God and died for their sins (1 Samuel 4:11–18).

This sin of the young men was very great in the LORD's sight. . . .

1 SAMUEL 2:17a

12

Start Your Engines

Mike's older brother Jared had been away at college for two whole months before he sent the letter he promised. "Dear Mickey," he began. Mike hated when people called him that—but for a change it sounded okay from his big brother.

The first part of the letter was about disgusting cafeteria food and enormous classes and stunning college women. Then Jared got a little more honest:

> *Mickey, there's a lot of drinking here. You can pray for me that I find friends. In high school I had friends who didn't drink. I live on a dorm wing with 29 other guys. It seems like all of them drink.*
>
> *I started going to a Bible study on campus. Good people there. Remember what Dad used to tell us when we were little and he went on business trips?* "Be strong and courageous, because God is with you." *That's helping me survive here. So many things are new. I still haven't found a part-time job. Some of the people here are really weird.*
>
> *I miss you. See you at Thanksgiving. Stay cool,*
>
> *Jared*

☛ Read James 1:4–6. How do you get ready to survive on your own?

There's only one road to maturity. It's full of potholes.

Imagine a world where your parents aren't standing ready to whip out the wallet. Where you decide *when* you study or *if* you study—or *when* you go to bed or *if* you go to bed. Where you can choose your friends, your enemies, your roomies, and your church—or none of the above. Where you can bake brownies for breakfast or inhale tater tots three times a day. Where $1.50 is a fortune and you have to decide if your clothes will survive a spin in the washer if you mix colors with whites—or maybe you decide never to wash them at all.

Welcome to life on your own.

You'll grow up fast then. But you're getting ready now. How you spend the next half dozen years determines whether you're prepared—or scared—to live on your own. Every rough spot in the road is a test. And every pothole you learn to steer around now is one less that can blow a tire later.

———

Perseverance must finish its work so that you may be mature and complete, not lacking anything.

James 1:4

PART 2

FINDIN' WINGS

13

Dad and Mom on Milk Cartons

Your teammates almost flatten you as they bound out of the locker room. Coach is sick, the assistant out of town. Practice canceled.

Your parents don't expect you home for two hours, so they'll never know you're not at practice. You have total freedom to slip away—to go anywhere, to do anything. Big question: What to do?

Bigger question: Who are you when your parents aren't around?

You spend quite a bit of your existence out of your parents' sight. But you never get out of their minds. They relax only when they know where you're going, what you're doing, and when you'll be home—and even then they're nervous. When you step out of their sight, you leap into another dimension: the danger zone.

You probably don't see it that way. You don't bow and scrape and thank your parents for the privileges of freedom. You just bolt. Being off on your own is no big deal.

Think again. It *is* a big deal.

✔ **Read Luke 2:42–52. What did Jesus do when He misplaced His parents?**

When Jesus' parents headed home from Jerusalem they traveled with a caravan of relatives. They as-

39

sumed He was somewhere with them.

Wrong.

After three days, Jesus no doubt had noticed Mary and Joseph had left without Him. But Jesus didn't exactly worry himself sick or pull down a cellular phone from heaven or paint Mom and Dad's poor lost faces on goatmilk cartons. He sat tight.

He was in the right place. He was doing the right thing.

Even when His parents weren't around.

Whenever you step out it's *your* job to look after yourself—where you're going and what you're doing. Part of that job is keeping your parents informed so they don't have nervous fits. But the even bigger part is watching out for their number one concern: you.

On our own not one of us is brilliant enough to always make wise choices. None of us are upstanding enough to always make right choices. But God is both wise and good. And He's promised to lead the way (Proverbs 3:5–7).

When his parents saw him, they were astonished.
His mother said to him, "Son, why have you treated
us like this? Your father and I have been
anxiously searching for you."
"Why were you searching for me?" he asked.
"Didn't you know I had to be in my Father's house?"

LUKE 2:48–49

14

Once Upon a Tractor

Dane sat in the tractor's enclosed cab, howling with the stereo. But when he finished plowing the back forty of the family farm, he quieted down and watched the sun set over the rich black fields. He told himself that maybe farming would be okay.

For eighth-grade graduation Dane had to give a speech describing what he would be doing ten years from now. Dane knew exactly what he was *supposed* to do—work the farm. Meeting each week with his youth pastor and going to a Bible study with 40 other kids, though, gave Dane other ideas. But he was afraid everyone would laugh if he told his real dreams. Besides that, Dane didn't want a blowup like the one his sister and her husband set off when they left the farm. He'd never seen Dad so mad. He said they were "chasing rainbows" or something like that.

It's just a stupid speech. Maybe he could make up a story about being a farmer. *It's not really a lie. I can't talk about being a youth pastor. Dad will kill me.*

✔ **Read Psalm 139:13–16. When is it okay to disagree with your parents?**

Your parents hold you to a routine meant to make you an Olympic swimmer, but you dream of being an

41

artist. You want to transplant brains, but your family tells you you're brainless. Your dad expects you to be his clone, but you'd sooner haul garbage. They laugh, they scold, and you get the message: conform or face the consequences.

Conformity can be good. Without parental pressure you would ditch school, make armpit noises during sermons, and whine like a baby when you don't get your way.

It would be wrong to obey your parents if they ever told you to do obvious evil (Acts 5:29). And it's wrong to disobey them when they tell you to do what's definitely right and good. But the solutions to some quarrels aren't that clear.

Your big wish might be to find out what you can get away with. But quiz yourself first: *Why* do you want to break the mold? *Who* do you want to please?

Your goal isn't to unnerve your parents or to pursue brathood but to run to what God wants. You're to listen to parents faithfully. But you're to obey God completely—and chase hard what He designed you to be. Your parents gave you birth, but God made you. You're His.

———

My frame was not hidden from you when I was made in the secret place. When I was woven together in the depths of the earth, your eyes saw my unformed body. All the days ordained for me were written in your book before one of them came to be.

PSALM 139:15–16

15
Tough Time

What was supposed to be a tame all-girl sleepover for Laura's birthday was getting hyper. Obnoxious. And worse. Therese and Jill hadn't planned to sleep much, but this was beyond their foggiest expectations.

Therese and Jill were just beginning to figure out that the frothy pink birthday punch wasn't causing the punchiness when a pack of guys from school tromped in. The girls glanced at each other. Without a word they knew it was time to leave—at three in the morning—and found a phone in a back bedroom. Jill's dad groaned like a bear wakened from hibernation, but as soon as Jill whispered the words "alcohol" and "boys" he said he would be right there.

Stares pierced the girls as they rolled up their sleeping bags and headed for the door. They stood outside in the cold, their best friends inside laughing at them—their *ex*-best friends, probably.

> Read 2 Timothy 1:7. You know you're supposed to resist peer fear. But how?

Nothing is scarier than facing a roomful of people who think you're a dork. Even if you want to be friends, something about you makes them hate you.

They might not like what you do. They might not like *you*.

You could talk like them, act like them, mangle people like them, smoke or drink or inhale like them—all to keep from looking stupid and feeling alone. You could give up and give in. You could suck up and let people control you.

Or you can stick with the Friend who sticks with you and let Him make you strong.

God promises that the same power that raised Christ from the dead lives inside you if you belong to Him (Romans 8:11). His Holy Spirit remakes you to want and to be able to do what's right. That's a "spirit of power" and a "spirit of self-discipline." But He also promises to make you able to face others with a "spirit of love." It's what made Jesus' first followers fearless and forgiving even when others hated them (Acts 6:8–8:2).

Following God doesn't make you timid. It makes you tough.

For God did not give us a spirit of timidity, but a spirit of power, of love and of self-discipline.

2 TIMOTHY 1:7

16

Too Good for Your Own Good

Jeremy and his science partner both torch holes in their desks with bunsen burners, but when smoke detectors begin to screech it isn't Jeremy who gets caught. "You're in charge, Jeremy," his teacher calls out as he escorts Jeremy's pyro pal to the principal's office. Jeremy congratulates himself on his promotion to teacher. *Not bad.*

After school Jeremy scores points at a quickmart by turning in his brother for shoplifting three candybars and a soda—for him. "Come back in a couple years and I'll give you a job, son," the manager says. Jeremy pats himself on the back. *Impressive.*

And that evening Jeremy's confirmation teacher frowns as she picks glass from the shattered classroom window. "We're going to sit here until someone claims responsibility," she scowls, "except for the girls—and Jeremy. You may go." Ever since Jeremy squealed on the kids smoking pot in the church basement everyone has assumed Jeremy was an angel. *I'm too good*, Jeremy thinks as he exits class.

📝 **Read Philippians 3:7–14. How do you know what a real Christian looks like?**

If you spend time with pigs you'll figure you're dirt-free. If all of your friends are as bright as sheep

45

you'll conclude you're brainy. If you hang out with dogs you'll think your breath smells minty fresh.

How you measure up all depends on what yardstick you use.

Comparing yourself to friends or enemies or kids at school or church doesn't really tell whether you're what God wants you to be. The Bible is your one yardstick. It alone sets God's standard (2 Timothy 3:16–17).

The tight friendship with God that Paul describes in Philippians isn't meant to be a standard you can't reach. God makes you acceptable to himself through Christ's death for your sins. He pries your eyelids open to see that He's more important than anything else in the world. And He helps you up when you stumble. Nothing could be more depressing than having to live up to perfection—the reputation of an older brother or sister with a gargantuan brain, or the trophies of a parent who was a champion *whatever*. But what God *wants* you to be He *helps* you to be.

I consider everything a loss compared to the surpassing greatness of knowing Christ Jesus my Lord, for whose sake I have lost all things. I consider them rubbish, that I may gain Christ and be found in him. . . .

PHILIPPIANS 3:8–9

17
Grumpy Burgers

"Emily, what's this?" Emily's boss holds open a cheeseburger. A line of ketchup forms a bright red smile, nicely set off by two blops of mustard for the eyes.

"That's a happy face."

"See the sign outside? This is *Grumpy Burgers*. We don't do happy faces."

"I was just being creative," Emily explains. "Don't customers get bored with food that looks the same every time?"

"No. It's burger, onion, cheese on top, pickle, ketchup, mustard. In that order. Squirt the ketchup here, ooze the mustard there. Got it? Or is that too hard for you?"

"I got it." Emily straightens her hat and for a while dresses burgers oh-so-properly—until boredom hits again. Instead of smiley faces she makes frowny faces.

"Emily!" her boss yells a few minutes later. "What—is *this*?"

Mr. Grumpy isn't amused.

☑ **Read Romans 13:1–7. Why would you want to do what people in charge say you should?**

If you work for a jerk you could drop burgers on the floor, spit in the soda, and blow your nose in the

47

French fry vat. Or if a teacher goes demented you could ditch school, break every rule, and work hard to make him or her look like a fool.

But think twice. Bosses hire and fire. Teachers give grades. Police have handcuffs, tasers, tear gas, and jail cells. Acting up can land you on the wrong side of the boss, the principal, or the law.

But dodging the punishment that authorities dispense on evildoers is only half of why the Bible says you should submit to them—why you should obey them, or accept the consequences if you ever have a right reason to disobey. Here's the other half: Authority is God's idea. He invented bosses, teachers, and police—and designed a world where bosses have bosses, teachers have principals, police have chiefs, and all answer to Him. Without leaders containing us we would clobber each other.

Sometimes bosses and other authorities go ballistic over ketchup blops. But the only thing worse than living in a world where everyone seems to boss you around would be living in a world where no one does.

Consequently, he who rebels against the authority is rebelling against what God has instituted, and those who do so will bring judgment on themselves. . . . Therefore, it is necessary to submit to the authorities, not only because of possible punishment but also because of conscience.

ROMANS 13:2, 5

18
Wax Worship

Jared ran to his house, flew to the family room, dug for the TV remote, and flipped on the cable sports channel.

It's true.

For the past half season Charlie Denton—everyone's favorite wide receiver of all time—had crumpled in fear of defensive lines. He dropped passes Jared's dog could have caught. And without Denton's usual stellar performance his team slid to last place. Denton kept claiming an old knee injury was bothering him.

But now Jared saw video clips of a dozen squad cars pulling up at Denton's home and police taking his hero into custody, then replay after replay of a press conference where Denton admitted to everything from drug addiction to fixing games.

Later that evening Jared ripped down all the Denton posters in his room and shredded them into tiny pieces—except for one. He kept that for a dartboard.

✔ **Read 2 Timothy 3:10–17. How do you pick a hero?**

Big and powerful people can make you do what they say. You may not like a president, but you listen. You have to follow, but you're no fan.

Other people don't need to *force* you to like them. They make you laugh. Or they're like superheroes in masks and tights out crushing evildoers. Or you dream of singing—or shooting hoops—or skiing—or skating—the way they do. They're too cool to contain your enthusiasm.

You don't sit down and decide who your heroes will be. You hear what others say, see who looks the prettiest, watch who scores the most. You don't use a checklist.

Maybe you should.

Paul listed all the reasons why Timothy should imitate him and heed what he said. Paul was real. He didn't set a record, get rich, get high, and kill himself six months later. His coolness lasted a lifetime, through victories and catastrophes.

Most pop heroes turn out to be wax figures who melt in the heat. It's usually the heroes close by—like parents, grandparents, teachers—who turn out to be eternal stars.

———————

But as for you, continue in what you have learned and have become convinced of, because you know those from whom you learned it. . . .

2 TIMOTHY 3:14

19
Saved From the Drain

Ellen sobbed and ran into the rest room. Steven, though, looked pleased with himself. What he said about Ellen was cruel—but good for a pack of laughs.

Julie was fed up with Steve's thermonuclear sarcasm. "You're a jerk. I hate the way you treat people. Can't you see what you did to Ellen? Don't you feel bad? What's wrong with you?"

Matt rushed to Steve's rescue. "Don't blame him. He can't help it. It's just the way he is. Mr. Jackson says it's his personality."

"Actually, it's his biochemistry," Megan suggested. "Perhaps Steve should see my psychiatrist for a prescription."

"What's wrong with *you*, girl?" Liz butted in. "He doesn't have ADD. He has SNOT—a sarcastic, nasty, obnoxious tongue. He needs to say he's sorry and glue those lips shut."

Read Ephesians 4:17–24. Can you help it if you're bad?

Sure, you might slip and bonk your head. Or you could be a small child and fall and not be able to rescue yourself. But otherwise it's tough to drown in a bathtub. If you drew a hot bath and lay there lazily until your skin wrinkled—and then soaked longer until your skin rotted—and then lingered in the tub still longer until one day you dissolved into nothing and whooshed down the drain—now that would be *your* fault.

Paul uses some big words in this passage to say that apart from God you want to stay stuck in a tub of sin. You lose your grip on what's right. You lounge in sin so long that your heart becomes numb with hatred, your mind dead with rebellion.

But God made a way for you to get unstuck. Christ lived so you could see what God is like; He died and rose so you could be made right with God. When you accept the fact that Christ rescued you, you want no more of sin (Titus 2:11–12). As you soak in God's truth—the Bible—you start to think differently. God works in you. You hate sin. You chase what's good. And it starts to show in how you act.

You get out of the tub before you wash down the drain.

You were taught, with regard to your former way of life, to put off your old self, which is being corrupted by its deceitful desires; to be made new in the attitude of your minds. . . .

EPHESIANS 4:22–23

20

Rattlesnake Hair

The only reason Luke dared join the chess club was that it met so early before school that no one knew he was in it—no one who mattered, anyway. Each morning he ducked out of the club meetings a few minutes early, snuck out the school's back entrance, and strode back in the front door. Perfect—until Miss Schaffhausen, the chess club sponsor, decided to take the club to after-school tournaments. Big problem: That's when Luke played on the school soccer team.

The team was good. They knew it. And next to soccer their favorite sport was kicking clods they didn't like—like anyone in the chess club. When Luke was with his soccer friends he set the team record for rude chesshead remarks.

And then one day after school two buses sat in the school driveway, both full of people hanging out the windows screaming at each other, both waiting for Luke to board.

Luke contemplated crawling under the wheels.

📝 **Read Proverbs 6:12–14. What price do you pay when you change to fit your surroundings?**

Before you go to battle in the desert you slip into sand-colored clothes and coil a rattlesnake around

53

your head. If you fight in the Arctic you sport snow-storm white and hang icicles from your nose. And for combat in the jungle you wear green and black fatigues complimented by face paint and twigs in your hair. It's simple survival.

If camouflage is good enough for the marines it's good enough for you. Right?

You'll change a lot more than your clothes if your social survival strategy is doing whatever it takes to fit, belong, blend in. You pretend to like stuff you hate and to detest stuff you love. You talk behind people's backs—out of both sides of your mouth. You get talked *into* and *out of.* And you chomp anyone you think resides lower on the food chain. With winks, nods, and inside jokes you're two-faced. Deceitful. A fraud.

But at least two people know the truth. You. And God. When you hide the real you no one can laugh at you. But neither can anyone truly like you.

A scoundrel and villain, who goes about with a corrupt mouth . . . who plots evil with deceit in his heart—he always stirs up dissension.

PROVERBS 6:12, 14

54

21

No More Doggy Bags

Falling back on her favorite humiliation/avoidance tactic, Sheena hung behind the backstop while everyone chose teams. Actually, she preferred baseball diamonds with dugouts or snack stands—more places to hide—but backstops worked in a pinch.

Those kids make me so mad! Sheena growled inside. *They always leave out the little ones.* When Sheena was little she always got picked last. When she got bigger she never got picked at all.

But now she could do something about it. What Sheena loved about her volunteer summer job at the park was helping the shy and small kids who got stomped on like she always did. She couldn't play ball—especially not with the kids who were almost her age—but she did know how to take the bunch who didn't get picked and start a whompin' good game of kickball.

Sheena glanced at the ball diamond and then at her little kickballers. They weren't leftovers. And neither was she.

📝 **Read Romans 12:3–8. We're all different—is that good or bad?**

You might glance around and conclude you're in a league by yourself. You're the first, the best, the greatest, the latest. *Too vain.* Or you might lean to the other extreme—you're a wretched slime, a leftover. *Downright warped.*

Your body wouldn't work if every part were the same. An ear can't see. An eye can't hear. You don't walk on your hands or eat with your feet. No part is better. None is a spare.

God put Christians together as the "body of Christ." We can't function without the gifts God packs into each of us—gifts of serving, teaching, leading, encouraging, and a bundle of other abilities. (Ephesians 4:11–16 and 1 Corinthians 12:4–11 list even more gifts.) And gifts don't just work in church. What God has built into you shows up at home, school, when you work, and with friends.

Slamming others because they lack the gifts you have is like hacking off your hand. And hiding who *you* are is like lashing your other behind your back. Neither is smart—unless you like to feed your face with your footsies.

We have different gifts, according to
the grace given us.

ROMANS 12:6

22
The Facts of Life

First question. *I know this one,* you reassure yourself. *X equals Y squared plus 4.* You plug in the numbers. No go. You try again. *X equals the square root of the inverse of Y.* El humungo blanko. Minutes pass. You're still stuck on the first test question. You chew the end off your pencil. You swallow the eraser.

Breathe. It's in there somewhere. You close your eyes, rock back and forth, and try to remember your teacher working the problem on the board. Your brain happily spits facts. *Abraham Lincoln. The spotted owl. December 7, 1941.*

You're not even hitting the right sector of the hard drive. You need one measly bit of data. It's lost. You freeze.

You know that as soon as you slap your blank test on the teacher's desk the misplaced factoids will come whooshing back. You consider slamming your head onto the desk. Maybe it'll crack open and leak brain onto your paper.

📝 **Read Mark 12:28–31. What one thing—two things, actually—does Jesus say you should remember about being His follower?**

Life is dazzling. Frazzling. You cram into your head things you'd better remember. Life skills. Test

57

stuff. Street smarts. Details about friends, fractions, and facial scrubs.

How do you keep it all straight?

Jesus sifted through the whole mix of life to get to two unforgettable thoughts. Number one: God is supreme. Perfect. Lord over all. He deserves everything in you. He's worth your following Him with all your heart, soul, mind, and strength. And number two: The people around you are yours to love with the same love you give yourself.

Those aren't the ignorable favorite thoughts of a math teacher who thinks that eighth-grade math holds the secrets of the universe. They're the ultimate commands of the Living God. You can forget a lot of stuff—but not these, the two great facts of life. Whether you're at home or out on your own, they remind you how to live.

When life squeezes, your brain freezes. But these facts are for the front burner.

———————

"The most important one," answered Jesus, "is this. . . . 'Love the Lord your God with all your heart and with all your soul and with all your mind and with all your strength.' The second is this: 'Love your neighbor as yourself.' "

MARK 12:29–31

23
Sure

"You used to be nice." Sasha rapped David on the head. "You're changing."

"Me? Changing?" David faked innocence. "I'm just not a dork anymore."

"At school you ignore me and everyone else from church," Sasha complained.

"Oh—" David fought back. "So you're jealous of my new friends."

Sasha didn't answer right away. "That's not the problem," she said after a long silence. "It's bigger than that. You ignore everything about being a Christian."

"So?"

"See? You act like it doesn't matter. I'm not sure who you are anymore. I thought you were a Christian."

"So did I," David finally admitted. "Now I'm not so sure."

▶ **Read Hebrews 10:19–23. How do you know that you're a Christian?**

Who you are is partly what you like. Partly the way you act. Partly how you feel. It's also what you believe. And most of all it's who you belong to.

We belong to God because He made us (Psalm 24:1–2). We belong to Him, that is, except we decided we didn't. We snubbed His kindness. We disobeyed His commands. We *all* chose not to follow God—we chose to sin, to do wrong again and again, to distance ourselves from Him (Romans 3:23). And the sentence God declares for sin is death—total, endless separation from Him (Romans 6:23).

The Old Testament pictured that separation concretely. God's presence dwelled in the temple, in the "Most Holy Place." Only one priest could pass through a curtain to get close to God's presence—and only once a year. And that high priest dared come close only if he carried the blood of an animal killed as a sacrifice for the people's sin (Leviticus 16).

But an animal can't take our place and die for our sins. God's Son—Jesus—did. He was the perfect sacrifice for all sins for all time. His blood opens a new way for us to "enter the Most Holy Place" with confidence. His death means God cleanses us, accepts us, and removes our guilt. No fear of eternal separation from God—just sureness of eternal life with Him that starts right now (John 3:16).

Becoming a Christian begins by saying, "Yes, God, I accept Christ's death for my sins. I admit I belong to you." You don't run from God anymore. You run toward Him. You don't choose to be far away. You choose to follow.

Let us draw near to God with a sincere heart in full assurance of faith, having our hearts sprinkled to cleanse us from a guilty conscience and having our bodies washed with pure water.

HEBREWS 10:22

PART 3

FLYIN'
HIGH

24

Look Out Below

From your perch atop your office tower—all 110 stories of it—you gaze at waves surging on the ocean beyond the city. Your ride to the top was quick. A little lawn-mowing service, a few lucrative investments, and *whammo*—you own a sizable chunk of the world.

You bought a city block. You built a building. It's yours. Downstairs you have a garage packed with cars—Beemers and Humvees and Ferraris. They're yours. And every one of the thousands of workers in the tower below answers to you. All yours.

Your feet? Propped up on the desk. Your nose? Sky-high. Your bank account? Bigger than the gross national product of Bulgaria. You call the shots. You run the show. You're your own boss.

And you're only thirteen.

Just wait until you move away from home.

📝 **Read John 12:25–26. Who runs your life when your parents aren't around?**

Someday you might perch at the tip of the tallest office tower in the world. But there still will be Someone above you.

Whether your kingdom consists of a bunkbed, half a bedroom, and a few videogames—or a dorm room, a microwave, and a '78 Honda—or cars, condos, corporations, techno-toys beyond imagination, and the largest CD collection in the world—you're not master of the universe. You don't even rule your own life.

There's no escape: You serve *somebody*. The Bible says you're a slave either to what's wrong or to what's right (Romans 6:19), either to death or to life (Romans 8:6), either to Satan or to God (Ephesians 2:1–10).

Trying to run your own life is like leaping off your office tower. You won't fly. Life without God is a death-spiral as sure as gravity. But to "hate" life and give yourself back to God—that means to stick close to Him, obeying His commands—sends you soaring.

Growing up isn't getting free to finally rule the roost. It's your chance to choose for yourself to follow Jesus—to fly with the real Master of the Universe.

Whoever serves me must follow me; and where I am, my servant also will be.

JOHN 12:26

25

To Die or to Die

"Quit stalling!" Tadd's friends push. "Get him!"

Tadd's friends had made a deal—a dare to get into their club. The test to join started out as a joke, but one by one Tadd's friends had done it and passed.

Tadd was the only one left. It was his turn to beat someone up for no reason—other than to join the group, that is. His friends got to choose whose head he would ram inside out.

They picked Pat.

"He won't even fight back," they reminded Tadd. "He's a wuss."

Tadd more or less agreed with them. Pat was the only boy in the school band who played the flute. *That might be okay*, Tadd thought, *if Pat didn't walk, talk, and giggle like a girl.* He *was* strange. But Tadd had known Pat since kindergarten. He didn't deserve this.

And now a bunch of people were waiting for Tadd's first punch.

☑ **Read Mark 8:31–38. What did Jesus say was the toughest thing about following Him?**

You're caught between a rock—and *the* Rock (Isaiah 26:4). You face humiliation and rejection if you ignore the demands of your friends. Yet you know God will be less than thrilled watching you do wrong and abuse yourself, others, and Him.

Either way you die. So what's the use of picking sides?

Jesus bluntly told His disciples—His followers—that for Him to obey God's plan would mean He would be mocked and killed on the cross. He was still determined to obey God.

And Jesus said that in the same way anyone who wants to follow Him must "deny himself" and "take up his cross." To follow Jesus is to swap your way for His way—completely. It's to obey Him even when it hurts—even when you feel like you've been pierced with nails and all you can do is twist in pain.

Daring to stick with Jesus sometimes feels like you've been hung up to die. Tough stuff. But Jesus promises that His way leads to life.

Then he called the crowd to him along with his disciples and said: "If anyone would come after me, he must deny himself and take up his cross and follow me."

MARK 8:34

26

The Shock in Their Eyes

Jill glanced up from her Bible study notes and paused, startled to see Shannon standing at the back of the room. A horde of shocked faces said the same thing: Why is *she* here?

Jill had met "Shannon the Sleaze Queen" at a track meet. Even with a hacker's cough, Shannon still ran fast. Shannon, in fact, ran around a lot, Jill had heard.

"Hi, Shannon!" Jill blurted. Shannon grabbed a seat and listened quietly. A girl next to her helped her follow along in her Bible. At the end of the evening, she talked to a few people and then slipped out the back.

Jill found her the next day at track practice. "Did you see how they looked at me?" Shannon asked. "I knew they wouldn't want me there."

"But it got better," Jill reminded her. Shannon nodded. "They were just surprised to see you at a Bible study. You were a little shocked too, weren't you?" Shannon had to admit she was—and that she felt welcome. And that she wanted to go back.

✍ **Read Mark 2:13–17. Who did Jesus choose to hang out with?**

Your photo doesn't have to be plastered on TV ads that scream, "Don't let this happen to you" or "This

67

is your brain on drugs" to be a wrongdoer. You don't have to be a sleaze queen or an ax murderer to have offended God. When you grasp that God is good and sin is evil and how totally repulsive *all* evil is to God— well, you can start to feel like rat chow.

Here's the good news: We walked away from God, but while we were still stuck in sin He took the first step toward us (Romans 5:8). He didn't make people get perfect before He would be their friend.

The religious leaders watching Jesus hated His friendliness toward sinners. They mocked His choice of a crooked tax collector to be His follower and despised His dinners with sinners. But those who sneered at Jesus for chumming with the bad guys were blind to their *own* badness.

They didn't think they needed a spiritual doctor, so they pushed Jesus away. They stayed sick. It was the ones who admitted they needed a spiritual doctor who let Jesus near and got well.

Jesus said to them, "It is not the healthy who need a doctor, but the sick. I have not come to call the righteous, but sinners."

MARK 2:17

68

27

You and the Beanstalk

"Klass, ve are here to make zis boy big and schtrong, to give him superhuman schpiritual schtrength, to make him a good Christian."

Strapped to a glistening steel operating table, Michael found that his church's Sunday school superintendent had a unique way of fixing anyone who goofed off in class. He waved his arm at Michael. "Yah," he said, "zis is vhat happens to boys who do not pay attention in Sunday school,

"Ve vill first sew shut hiss big mouth.

"Next, ve will give him bigger ears—zo he listens.

"Ve will place tiny bits of tape above ze eyes to keep zem open. And zen—and zis is important—ve will inject him with special solution to make him schpiritually alert.

"Any qvestions?"

☑ **Read Mark 4:1–9 and 15–20. What makes a Christian strong?**

Growing spiritually brawny or beautiful doesn't mean you never get bored in Sunday school or snooze during a sermon or forget to read your Bible. But if you want to get closer to Christ, it shows in how hard you listen.

How you respond to Jesus resembles the way seed grows—or doesn't—when it lands on different dirts. The word of God—the message of His care for us, Christ's death for us, and His commands for us—is like seed. Like a farmer, God flings seed in all directions. Some drops on hard paths, where it settles on the surface and is snatched away. Other seed lands in rocky outcroppings. The seed springs up but dies for lack of roots, unable to reach water in the heat. Still other seed grows up among thorns—worries and distractions that choke a young plant.

But some seed falls on good soil—on those who pay attention to God's words, accept them, and act on them. Their lives explode with growth, producing a hundred times the amount of the first seed.

Each time you hear God's Word it's your chance to be rich, dark dirt. You can choose to listen or not, believe or not, obey or not. Live up to what you know and you'll grow. Don't and you won't.

Other seed fell on good soil. It came up, grew and produced a crop, multiplying thirty, sixty, or even a hundred times.

· MARK 4:8

28

A Crying Game

100 yards. 5-iron if I'm lucky. You tee up the ball. *This time I'm going to put it on the green. I'm sick of them making fun of me.*

Smack! *Sounded nice.* But the ball hooks into the woods lining the fairway. *For sure I'll never find that one.* Your friends snicker.

You blush. "I'll take another one."

You top the ball and it dribbles fifty yards into a stream. You stuff back a scream. Your friends grew up on this course with their father, Mr. Golf Instructor. They're practically pros. You? Once again you're wondering why you golf with them.

This ball-in-water situation, however, you know how to handle. You've watched golf on TV. Real golfers hit it out. With both feet in six inches of stream, you swing hard. *Swash.* You connect—with the water. The ball that went in doesn't come out. The splash that goes up comes down. All over you. Your golf partners say you're stupid.

▶ **Read Matthew 4:1–11. Did Jesus ever struggle to do well at doing right?**

Here's how we picture this passage: Devil pounces. Jesus flexes muscles. Jesus flashes an orthodontically flawless smile. Jesus fires Scripture bits at devil. Devil whimpers away in defeat. Temptation bounces off Jesus like a bullet off Superman's chest. No fuss, no agony, not even a wrinkle in Jesus' tights.

That isn't how it happened.

Jesus hadn't eaten for 40 days. He fought temptation the same way we have to—the hard way—by clinging to the truth in a fight of faith. Satan didn't tempt Jesus with trinkets and a toy crown. He offered to make Jesus king of the world. And Satan didn't depart for good (Luke 4:13). The battle went on. Before Jesus went to the cross, for example, He asked His Father whether there was an easier way to save the world (Luke 22:41–46).

Struggling against temptation never feels good. When the temptation bullet comes your way, it hits, rips, rattles around inside, and goes out the back. But Jesus knew hurt. He understands your hurt. When He sees you struggle, He doesn't sneer, snicker, stand by and do nothing, or fake a pout with a big lip and crying eyes. He wades in to help (Hebrews 4:16).

Then Jesus was led by the Spirit into the desert to be tempted by the devil.

MATTHEW 4:1

29
Pop Quiz

Mom and Dad looked sympathetic. "We know how you feel, Hanna," they explained. "But we don't have any choice about moving. It will be okay. God's going with us, you know. You'll see."

I'm going to die, Hanna thought. *It's not even summer. If we have to move, why do we have to do it in the middle of the year?*

While Hanna's family packed up their stuff and she said goodbyes to her friends, she hatched a plan. She'd walk to school so no one would see her sitting by herself on the bus. At the new school she'd dart from class to class—if she walked fast and looked like she knew where she was going then no one would notice she was totally friendless. She'd skip lunch and hide in a corner of the library.

She steeled herself to face a new school all alone. *God?* she said to herself. *What does He care?*

📝 **Read John 6:5–13. What does God really want from us?**

Situation comes up. A crowd of 5,000 men—plus women and children—swarms toward Jesus and His disciples. Jesus sees it's time to eat. And time for a pop quiz: "Where's lunch coming from?" Jesus asks. "For the whole hillside!" He adds. But He's not wondering where He can find the nearest Taco Tom's or looking for volunteers to cough up a spare year of salary. What He really wants is to know what the disciples think about Him.

None of Jesus' disciples answers the quiz question right. Philip mumbles about the price. Andrew finds a kid toting what he regards as a useless little snack of fish and chips. The disciples all think Jesus means the lunch problem is *their* problem. To solve. To survive. And on their own they don't see solutions.

All Jesus wants them to do is to ask for His help. "Crack the bread in half, Jesus," He wants them to say. "Start passing it around. You're able to do what we can't." What He wants from His disciples—from His followers back then and from us now—is trust. It wasn't supposed to be a trick question. It was a trust question.

When Jesus looked up and saw a great crowd coming toward him, he said to Philip, "Where shall we buy bread for these people to eat?" He asked this only to test him, for he already had in mind what he was going to do.

JOHN 6:5–6

30
God in a Box

You and your lab-coated friends gloat over your victim, awed by your own genius.

"It still looks strong," one worries. "Think the cage will hold?"

"The cage is fine." Another friend pokes it with a stick. "Look—it hardly moves. We got it good." You'd spent months stalking your victim. But capturing and caging it was only the first step of your plan.

The next step was to put its cosmic powers in a portable package.

Two friends twiddle the dials on the transmogrifier. One question left—how small to shrink your victim. Six inches high and it would fit in a box. A foot high and you could lead it around on a leash.

But before you can make a final decision, the phone rings. "It's someone who says *He's* God. It sounds for real."

"We've made a mistake," you mumble. "What we've got in the cage isn't God."

📝 **Read Mark 6:45–52. Why trust Jesus?**

Jesus had just taken a small sack of groceries, multiplied it, and fed some 10,000 people. Major miracle, yet the disciples didn't get it. This time Jesus strolls to their boat across the waves. *That can't be Jesus*, they think. They imagine He's a ghost. He reaches them and the wind dies down. The disciples are bewildered.

They still didn't get it. They had Jesus in a too-tight box. They didn't figure out His real identity. They couldn't fathom His power over *everything*. When He did things only God could do they stayed clueless. Sure, they knew Jesus was a cut above them. But He was *infinitely* greater. He was God himself, all-powerful, come to earth as a human being.

Power alone, though, doesn't make Jesus a hero. You'd fear Him if He threatened to evaporate you with a blast from His finger—or to detach your nose and ears with His bare hands. You wouldn't willingly like, love, or obey Him.

But Jesus is total power paired with perfect goodness. That's what makes Him worth trusting. He isn't just able to feed the crowds. He offers bread that satisfies forever (John 6:35). He doesn't just walk on water. He's the One who says, "It's me! Don't be scared!"

———————

But when they saw him walking on the lake, they thought he was a ghost. They cried out, because they all saw him and were terrified. Immediately he spoke to them and said, "Take courage! It is I. Don't be afraid."

Mark 6:49–50

31
Booked Solid

"I can't—really," Tina protested. "Here—look at my calendar." Tina popped open her locker and flopped out a scheduler. Mary flipped through month by month. Tuesday—the night Mary's youth group met—was scribbled full for weeks.

"See?" Tina poked at the Tuesdays. "I volunteer at the nursing home every Tuesday evening for the next eight weeks. I'll put you down for February 17."

Mary counted on her fingers. "That's 12 weeks."

"I help at Children's Hospital two Tuesdays after that," Tina explained, "and I need to keep a couple weeks open for emergencies. Good time management."

"Sure," Mary said. "I understand. You'd just said you wanted to come to a Bible study sometime. You know—all those questions you had when your grandpa died. We have stuff on other nights sometimes."

"Sorry!" Tina apologized. "It wouldn't matter. I'm booked solid."

☑ **Read Matthew 19:16–22. What kept the young man from following Jesus?**

Jesus didn't insist you had to be poor. He *did* say there are lots of things more important than having

77

lots of things (Matthew 6:19–34.) He didn't imply God will accept you more quickly if you give away your camel. After all, you become God's friend not because of what *you do* but because of what *Jesus did.* Obeying lets you *experience* God's care, not buy it.

Yet Jesus pointed out that what the young man possessed owned him. He had done everything right—except love God above anything else. The man didn't strangle anyone, steal anything, or spew at his mother. But when Jesus invited him to follow—yet to ditch his luggage first—he couldn't bear to leave his horde of wealth behind.

Lots of things in life are good. But they aren't good anymore if they go extreme and keep you from following Jesus—like trying too hard to be popular (Galatians 1:10), overestimating the size of your brain (1 Corinthians 1:28–29), doing what's right—but to show off for others (Matthew 6:2–4), or getting too busy for God (Luke 10:40–42).

To follow Jesus, you have to let go of what's good when it keeps you from grabbing what's best.

Jesus answered, "If you want to be perfect, go, sell your possessions and give to the poor, and you will have treasure in heaven. Then come, follow me."

MATTHEW 19:21

32
Deepest Regrets

"Mitch is a Jesus-lover!" Scott taunts. "Christians are wusses. That's why Mitch won't kick butt and win."

Mitch knew he dug as hard as any other player on his hockey team. He just didn't love to break opponents' legs to stop shots. Besides, Scott was covering up for all the shots *he* woofed. But that didn't stop the team from joining Scott in pouncing on Mitch.

"It's true. He prays at lunch." *How could he tell? Mitch wonders. I don't stand up and yodel.*

"And he reads a Bible in the library." *Not that much. . . .*

"It's why he's a suck-up to all the teachers." *A suck-up? I just pay attention.*

"So?" Mitch finally speaks up. "Those things don't make me a Christian." *Well, technically not—they don't* make *me a Christian. But I do them because I'm a Christian.*

The dodge doesn't distract them. They stare him down. "So are you or aren't you?"

📭 **Read Luke 22:54–62. What did Peter do when people accused him of being Jesus' friend?**

If you follow Jesus, sooner or later people figure it out.

79

And sooner or later someone doesn't like it. They laugh at you or slam you or just ignore you.

You don't have to hang yourself out for them to hate you. The Bible doesn't say, "Go ye forth and rubbeth thy faith in thy neighbor's face." But it does coach you to be honest and unashamed: "Live such good lives among the pagans that, though they accuse you of doing wrong, they may see your good deeds and glorify God. . . ." (1 Peter 2:12).

Those are words from the guy who three times said he didn't know Jesus—only hours after he swore he would go with Jesus to prison and death (Luke 22:31–34).

Soldiers had swept in and captured Jesus, who would soon die. Like a cornered dog, Peter lashed out. He flashed a sword and whacked off a servant's ear (John 18:10). He feared for his own life and tried to hide. Then, just as Jesus had predicted, Peter claimed three times not to know Him.

One look from Jesus was enough for Peter to understand what he had done.

The Lord turned and looked straight at Peter. Then Peter remembered the word the Lord had spoken to him: "Before the rooster crows today, you will disown me three times." And he went outside and wept bitterly.

LUKE 22:61–62

33

Sob Stories

Adrianna buried her face in her pillow. *Sobs.*

She could count her close Christian friends on her two big toes after her church's third youth pastor in four years resigned and her youth group imploded. *Lonely sobs.*

Everyone she knew was into school or sports. She liked drama and music. Her social life was pathetic. *Bored sobs.*

One of her best friends even quit coming to church after a pastor told him that "following Jesus" was optional for Christians. Adrianna kept telling herself what she'd memorized from 2 Timothy 2:22— to "*pursue* righteousness, faith, love and peace, along with those who call on the Lord out of a pure heart." But where was everyone else? *Angry sobs.*

And she'd heard that the guy she liked at church thought of her as his sister. Barf. She'd uncovered a profound truth: No one ever asks his sister to a movie. Not that her parents would let her go. But it would be nice to be asked. *Shattered heart sobs.*

☑ **Read Matthew 11:28–30. How do you keep following Jesus when you feel like quitting?**

Life as an ox is tough. You eat slop from a pail. You sleep in a teeny stall. Then your owner pairs you with another clumsy animal, chunks a wooden yoke across your neck, and fastens you in. And it's drag the plow, pull the wagon—acre after acre, day after day.

Jesus invites you to take His yoke. But He won't treat you like an ox. You don't have to be brawny to pair up with Jesus. He wants you if you're weary. You can tell Him you're tired. You can cry. You can crab.

Jesus is Lord. He decides where to plow: He points you "in paths of righteousness for his name's sake" (Psalm 23:3). But He helps you to pull: "For it is God who works in you to will and to act according to his good purpose" (Philippians 2:13). And He'll lead you to places you can't believe: He is "able to do immeasurably more than all we ask or imagine, according to his power that is at work within us" (Ephesians 3:20).

And what He promises isn't slop and slavery. It's rest.

———————

Take my yoke upon you and learn from me, for I am gentle and humble in heart, and you will find rest for your souls. For my yoke is easy and my burden is light."

Matthew 11:29–30

34

Fairy Tales and Grave Dust

Rick acted like he knew a lot and Marie was stupid. "It's a myth, you know—all that junk about Jesus rising from the dead," he argued. "People invented God when they didn't understand stuff like evolution—or astrophysics."

"Astrophysics?" Ben pondered out loud. "Isn't that the dog on *The Jetsons*?"

"No, stupid," Rick spat. "That's *Astro*. Astrophysics is the study of bodies in space. Before you could have evolution you had to have stars and planets. Some people say it's okay to believe in Jesus—that He 'lives in our hearts.' You just can't say He's alive. He's dead. He's just a dead teacher. Like Mr. Zalinki."

"Dead like Mr. Zalinki," Ben grinned. "Good one, Rick."

"Where do you get this stuff?" Marie objected. "You can say Santa Claus and my Grandma Estelle 'live in my heart.' Jesus did more than that. He rose from the dead. Really. Body and all."

Read Luke 24:36–49. Why does it matter that Jesus isn't dust in a grave?

If Christ wasn't raised, Paul wrote, our faith is useless (1 Corinthians 15:14, 17). And His early followers knew it. After Jesus was crucified, they hid in fear. They'd hoped Jesus would set up the new kingdom He had promised. But then He was dead. Nothing had turned out how they had expected. A few disciples claimed He was alive. They said that the grave was empty. He'd risen from the dead (Luke 24:6, 34).

It seemed too good to be true—until Jesus suddenly stood among them.

Jesus dared them to study the scars on His hands and His feet where He had been nailed to the cross. He dined on a piece of fish. Jesus was no ghost, no figment from their wishes. He helped them understand that God had promised His resurrection all along.

So why does it matter?

By raising Jesus from the dead, God declared Jesus to be His Son (Romans 1:4). He confirmed that Jesus had paid in full for our sins (Romans 4:25). And get this: Because death couldn't keep Jesus in the grave, it won't keep His followers there either. He lives with us now. We'll live with Him forever.

He lived for real. He died for real. He rose for real. So we can follow Him for real. Now and forever.

"This is what is written: The Christ will suffer and rise from the dead on the third day, and repentance and forgiveness of sins will be preached in his name to all nations, beginning at Jerusalem. You are witnesses of these things."

LUKE 24:46–48

PART 4

SOARIN' HOME

35
Are We There Yet?

"You're on my side!" your little sister whines, swinging her Barbie at you. *Whack!* The hard plastic head cracks you across the nose.

"OW!" you howl. "Stop it! MOM—that HURT! Make her stop!"

The backseat of the family car has gotten way too tight on a trip that won't quit. You've been riding for weeks. Each evening you write in your journal about *The Great American Roadtrip*—under "things I'd rather forget."

"This is so stupid!" you fuss. "Where are we going?"

Your parents don't disclose your destination. They won't trace on a map the route you're taking. "It's a surprise," they say.

One day you stop at a gas station. The clerk is nosy in a friendly sort of way. "You folks aren't from around here, are ya," she figures. "Where ya headed?"

"Wish I knew," you reply. "Ask them. This was their idea."

📖 **Read Philippians 1:1–11. Where is Jesus taking you as you follow Him?**

You won't enjoy a long roadtrip if you haven't a clue where you're headed. If all you're sure of is that

87

your backside is glued to a carseat you'll feel duped, dragged to who-knows-where. And you'll yawn, snooze, and snore if you finally get to your destination and no one explains what you're looking at.

The White House is more than a house. The Grand Canyon is more than a hole in the ground. Following Christ is an adventure. But not understanding where you're headed—and why—and what you'll see along the way—turns the ride into a chore and a bore.

Paul flips through some postcards to show us our destination—actually, to show us what *we* will look like when our journey is done: Our relationship with Christ will change us completely. We'll be "pure," "blameless," "filled with the fruit of righteousness." Our lives will glow with God. People will see what He's done in us and worship Him. And on our trip we'll stick together and learn how to live best.

The trip has already begun. God is in the driver's seat. He promises to get us to the goal. And we don't have to guess where we're going.

He who began a good work in you will carry it on to completion until the day of Christ Jesus.

PHILIPPIANS 1:6

36

Don't Waste Yourself

Brandon had made sure everyone knew: No socks or underwear this year. Just cash. *I hope they put the money they saved on bows and paper into the card.* A card from his parents. *Cash!* One from Aunt Bertha. *Cash!* He rips into the rest. *Cash! Cash! Cash!*

In the end, Brandon has more money than he'd ever assembled in one spot, a tad more than the $128.38 he needed for a new video game deck.

Brandon heads for the mall but stalls at a carnival that had landed outside. He spots a toss-the-football-through-the-tire game with you-know-what as a prize: the game deck. Twelve misses later Brandon goes a few rounds on the *Whirl and Hurl* ride to prove he's still a real man. Brandon finally steps into the mall, only to realize he no longer has enough money for the game deck.

He panics. Before he knows what happened, he's outside the store staring into a bag stuffed with a ThighMaster and a 67-piece ice-fishing ensemble autographed by Wayne the Walleye Guy.

He's broke. And not too bright.

> **Read Proverbs 2:1–11. What good is God's wisdom?**

If you dash through a mall with a wad of ones, fives, tens, and twenties bulging in your pocket—

noseprinting windows, testing toys, trying on clothes, all with no plan of action—you might as well wear a button that says, "Rob me. I'm stupid." It's better to think, pray, decide, and attack. Get distracted and you'll be disappointed. Choose on the fly and later you'll regret it.

Your life is a lot more valuable than any birthday horde or your savings from mowing lawns or sitting babies. God wants you to spend your life well.

He won't leave you to panic. If you cry out for understanding, He'll give you all you need: "wisdom" (an ability to live skillfully), "knowledge" (brain capacity and insight into right and wrong), and "discretion" (being able to pick rightly between two actions or ideas). He'll keep you from wasting yourself in the mall of life.

For the LORD gives wisdom, and from his mouth come knowledge and understanding. He holds victory in store for the upright, he is a shield to those whose walk is blameless. . . .

PROVERBS 2:6–7

37
Caught Again

"We take these reports *very* seriously," Keri's school counselor scolded. Keri thought back to her essay on "What I want to be when I grow up." What did she write that got her handcuffed to a chair and wired to a lie detector? Why the blinding lights?

"We're not talking career, dear," her counselor continued. "This goes much deeper than that. In response to the question 'Would you rather be good, bad, or ugly?' you wrote 'I want to be good.' Really now, Miss Bratvold. Do you mean that? HMMM?"

"Yes," Keri stammered. "Yes, I do."

"I'm sure you do," her counselor sneered. "But there's this little matter of cheating. We know that you peeked at Tim Ford's math homework back in third grade."

Keri gasped. "I didn't mean to!"

"And just last week—did you or did you not make rude and false remarks about Lindsey Rich?" her counselor pressed. Keri started to cry. "Need I continue?" inquired her counselor. We have a *long* list of instances when you were in fact *not* good."

☑ **Read Romans 7:21–25. What's your problem when you can't seem to do what's right?**

Blinded by a spotlight, cuffed like a criminal, plugged in to a lie detector—forced to be honest—

91

none of us has a shortage of shortcomings. We know the rules well. Yet we fail to keep them perfectly—no matter how hard we try.

It's like an annoying hunk of hair that always curls the wrong way. Slick it down, mousse it up, as soon as you drop your guard: *fuh-wang!* Some of the curls in our character, though, aren't small. And they matter even more than doofy hair.

Even after we've decided to follow Jesus, sin still hounds us (Hebrews 12:1). Part of us wants to do what's right. Part of us doesn't. We can blame others, make excuses, or hide our faults, but it always comes back to one fact: there's something wrong with *us*. We're at war within ourselves.

But admitting we're a tangled mess opens the way for God to fix us. Being a Christian isn't just knowing the rules. It's not even knowing when you've broken them. It's relying on the Master.

———————

What a wretched man I am! Who will rescue me from this body of death? Thanks be to God—through Jesus Christ our Lord! So then, I myself in my mind am a slave to God's law, but in the sinful nature a slave to the law of sin.

Romans 7:24–25

38

The Un-Christian

"It's okay," Norman sighs, unfurling his homework after the neighbor's cat ate it and hacked it up four days later like a hairball. "It was due yesterday, but at least I'll have something to turn in." Such was Norman's life.

When Norman goes to school the next day, he finds his principal has thrown everything out of his locker and given it to a new kid. "It's just what I would have done," Norman sighs. And when he goes to English class, he finds the new kid has taken his desk. "I'll sit up front on the floor. It's cold and hard, but I'll be fine."

"Don't be dense, Norman," remarks Norman's teacher. "The custodians can bring in another desk."

And after school Norman discovers his dog has been run over by a car, his parents kidnapped by terrorists, and his house blown up by the bully across the street.

"Oh well," Norman sighs. "It's okay. Really it is."

Read Romans 8:9–17. What does it matter that God's Spirit lives in you?

As you become more and more like Jesus, you don't exactly become less and less like you. God doesn't erase your personality. He doesn't overwhelm your emotions with perpetual bliss and good cheer. He doesn't vacuum out your brain. And He doesn't convert you into a satellite-guided RoboChristian that acts holy at the flip of some heavenly switch.

You still feel. You still think. You still react. You still act.

Here's what really happens. You've recognized that you belong to God. You've accepted His forgiveness. You have a new relationship with the God of the Universe. You no longer dread God. You can, in fact, call Him "Abba" ("Father," or even "Daddy"). He isn't simply "out there" somewhere. You now have God himself living *in* you through His Spirit.

The Bible says the Spirit lives through you (Galatians 2:20). He produces love, joy, peace, patience, kindness, goodness, faithfulness, gentleness, and self-control in you (Galatians 5:22–23). He helps you understand God's commands.

And as you listen and obey, the part of you that hates God's ways dies away.

————————

And if the Spirit of him who raised Jesus from the dead is living in you, he who raised Christ from the dead will also give life to your mortal bodies through his Spirit, who lives in you.

ROMANS 8:11

39

Big Baby

Steffi got claustrophobic every time she heard it. Whenever she wondered out loud why she had to go to church, her mom tossed her the same line: "Because it's right! We go to church because it's the right thing to do."

To Steffi, "the right thing to do" was excruciatingly, painfully, agonizingly boring. She'd tried everything to escape. Some Sundays she screamed. Other Sundays she shot cold, ugly stares at her mom. And one Sunday she yanked the covers over her head and ignored her mom. (Bad choice. Steffi disliked going to church. She *really* disliked getting dragged from bed and going to church with her hair and face gnarled.)

Steffi wanted a real reason to show up at Sunday school and to sit through a church service—something more than a "just because."

Somehow Steffi's mom always won.

But pretty soon Steffi would be too big to be carried to the car and strapped in the seat belt.

📝 **Read Psalm 95:1–11. What does it mean to "worship" God?**

When you follow God, He begins to build five things inside of you: *worship* toward Him, *humility* toward yourself, and *love* toward others, all kept sharp by *commitment* to do right and *honesty* when you've done wrong.

God is all-powerful: Lord, Master, Judge. God is all-kind: the Giver of forgiveness through Christ. But if you don't perceive God's mind-boggling perfection then humility, love, commitment, and honesty don't make sense. Being a Christian becomes rules and ritual—just the right thing to do—rather than a relationship with your God.

God himself is the reason behind everything you do as a Christian. And church is one chance to bow before Him. Your *mouth* worships. You tell God how great He is. You "shout aloud to the Rock," the one who rescues you from sin's power and penalty. No mumbling meaningless words, though—your *heart* worships too. You acknowledge that you belong to God. You agree that His will is good. And you worship with your *life*, giving yourself to Him out of thankfulness for what He's done for you (Romans 12:1).

God doesn't drag you to church. He wants you to grasp His greatness.

Come, let us bow down in worship, let us kneel before the LORD our Maker; for he is our God and we are the people of his pasture, the flock under his care.

PSALM 95:6–7

40

Who's the Leader of the Band?

"You deserve it, dear," Tonya's mother coos. "Just push your way up to the front. It's where you belong. If you're ever going to win the Teenage Miss Minnesota contest, you *have* to be in the front. Do you think those judges would pick a girl who just stands in the back?"

The next day at the gymnastics team photo eleven girls wait for instructions. *This'll be in the paper—* Tonya thinks—*and the yearbook—and plastered in the school showcase by the trophies.* Tonya inches forward. *And my entry! I've got to get to the front.*

Tonya pushes past the others and drops into the splits. *Idiots. They're just standing there. They don't know what really matters.*

Tonya's coach shakes her head. "Tonya, I want Linda to be the one in front."

"No!" Tonya protests. "Me! Me! Me! I *have* to be in *front!*"

📝 **Read Mark 9:33–37. What does someone who possesses "humility" look like?**

"What were you arguing about?" Jesus asked politely.

He knew.

"Nothing," they blushed. "It's not important."

Jesus had just told His disciples He would be killed. Not that He'd get a star on Hollywood's Sunset Boulevard. Not that He'd received invites to all the hot talk shows. Not that He and His band would play to packed stadiums on a sellout world tour.

He would soon be crucified.

You'd think the disciples would have understood that being the world's Savior—or being His follower—wasn't a glamorous job.

Jesus told His disciples that following Him isn't about pushing yourself to the front of the crowd. To be first is to be last. But to be like Him is to welcome the ones people label "nerds" and "rug rats" and "pests." To imitate Him is to serve—even to suffer—to bring others life (Matthew 20:26–28).

Jesus was God himself (John 1:14). But He didn't push His way to the front. He was no brat.

———————

Sitting down, Jesus called the Twelve and said, "If anyone wants to be first, he must be the very last, and the servant of all."

MARK 9:35

41

Havenots

"It's simple, Mom." Julie tried to talk slowly so her mom could understand. "I have more important things to do than clean my room. Would *God* like it if I blew my lesson?"

Tomorrow was Julie's turn to teach the three-year-olds in Sunday school. She still had to write out a story, practice a song, and make a craft. She did need to start. The lesson did have to get done. But Julie acted like she'd been slaving all week long.

"What's the lesson on?" Mom asked.

"Love."

"Your lesson is going to sound pretty hypocritical. You know, Julie, I asked you to pick up your room and help your brother with his math."

"What does that have to do with anything?"

"It's about love and respect," Mom grimaced. "You're supposed to teach about love and you're acting just the opposite. I don't think God likes that either."

📝 **Read 1 Corinthians 13:1–8. What is love?**

If someone gave you a bazillion dollars, it would quake your world. You'd count it, roll in it, and wallpaper your room with it. What else? You'd be a jerk not to share it.

God has loved you with a heart-shaking love. What He pours into you He wants you to pour into others (1 John 4:19). But the love you show others isn't an act. It isn't *looking* good. It isn't even just *doing* good. God wants to work in you to enable you to *be* good from the heart.

Paul said that you can be sensational—utter God's words, pump mountains from place to place, or get burned at the stake for your faith—yet still not act out of love. You can teach toddlers or memorize the Bible or preach to thousands at a megawhopper church. But those aren't the same as spiritual maturity—a closeness to God you demonstrate in the steadiness of your loving thoughts and actions.

Love is such a huge part of who God is that the Bible says simply that "God is love." And it's such a big part of who His followers are that whether or not you love shows whether or not you know Him (1 John 4:7–8).

———————

If I give all I possess to the poor and surrender my body to the flames, but have not love, I gain nothing.

1 Corinthians 13:3

42

Stayin' Alive

"These—they're cool. Get some." Micah grabbed a shoe off the shelf and shoved it in Eric's face. Eric peered at the price sticker inside the heel and put the shoe down. "My parents said they'll only pay half. I have to save the rest."

"So you're gonna wait?" Micah scoffed.

"I *have* to wait. I only have half of my half. Are *you* going to pay for them?"

Micah pointed at his own shoes. "How do you think I got these?" Eric shrugged. "I put them on and walked out." Micah started to rummage through the shoe boxes under the display. "What size you want?"

Eric grabbed Micah's arm to stop his digging. "What about my parents? I'd get three feet inside the house and they'd want to know where I got them."

"Your parents don't have to see them," Micah reasoned. "Stick them in your locker and change at school. Make up your mind. You want the shoes or not?"

☑ **Read Romans 6:11–14.** *When* **do you decide to ditch evil?**

Some guy with biceps bigger than your whole head tries to drag you into a boxing ring to knock your block off. What's the best strategy to stay safe? (a) throw a right jab and a left hook and hope you don't break your hand; (b) jump on the guy's back and attempt to rip his ear off; (c) bark like a seal to arouse pity; (d) stay out of the ring in the first place.

Smart choice.

Just before the passage you read, Paul tells the Romans that all Christians have "died with Christ." When you became a Christian—whether that process was quick, slow, yesterday, or a long time ago—God acted in you. Christ died *for* your sin, but you also died with Christ *to* sin. You said "No!" to evil. Besides that, God brought you "from death to life." God raised you with Christ, forgiving you, wiping your conscience clean, giving you a heart that's alive toward Him.

Here's the point: You died to sin—so stay dead. You committed yourself to following God—so grow in that commitment to Him. You made up your mind back then to ditch evil—so keep it made up. You decided to get out of the ring—so stay out.

———————

Do not offer the parts of your body to sin, as instruments of wickedness, but rather offer yourselves to God, as those who have been brought from death to life; and offer the parts of your body to him as instruments of righteousness.

ROMANS 6:13

43

Lumberjacks on Ice

You and your friend look like lumberjacks-turned-surfer-dudes as you trudge across the street in your flannel and baggies outfits, headed for the neighborhood hill.

With snowboards swung across your backs you're a little slow. Too tardy for the guy in the Corvette waiting at a light to make a right turn. He honks. *What's his problem?* He guns the engine and edges forward. As he turns behind you he nicks your friend's board and breezes your leg.

You pick up a hunk of ice and wing it at the Vette's back end.

Chink! Ice connects with window. No damage. But driver skids to stop. Driver blasts into reverse. Grinds to stop. Exits car. Chases snowboarders. Cop sees chase. Cop prevents your premature deaths. *Good thing.* Cop totally blames hip kids. *Bad thing.*

You find yourself in the backseat of a police car on the way home. The officer phones ahead. Your parents greet you at the door.

📖 **Read Psalm 139:23–24. Why be honest?**

You blew it. You were caught in the act. Or you're at least the prime suspect.

What's your first reaction to accusation?

Your gut no doubt tells you to flee like a prisoner who knows that the guards are snoozing. You try to tunnel out and sneak away. Or you blow a hole in the prison wall and tell a bold, bald lie. You point out the evil someone else committed and cover up what you did. You rave about the driver who went psycho but subtract from your story the ice hunk you flung.

None of us likes to be wrong. It's easy to tell less than the whole truth. But when God wants to lead you into *worship* toward Him, *humility* toward yourself, *love* toward others, and a *commitment* to do right in all circumstances—then *honesty* when you've sinned is what keeps you stuck close to him. Dodging truth leaves you dead toward God (1 Thessalonians 2:10).

God knows the whole story—what you've done and what you haven't. And if you ask Him, He'll help you be honest with Him, yourself, and other people. He'll show you *you*—no better, no worse. He'll help you admit your part—no more, no less.

Search me, O God, and know my heart; test me and know my anxious thoughts. See if there is any offensive way in me, and lead me in the way everlasting.

PSALM 139:23–24

44
Monkey Pile

"One-monkey! Two-monkey!" Josh counted. Then he rushed. *Bam!* Ben lay flattened, walloped in a quarterback sack.

Ben jumped up and pounced back at Josh. "Stop it! One more time and I'm quitting! It's *three* monkeys."

Josh laughed at Ben. "Benny's such a baby," he taunted.

Next play. "One-monkey! Two-monkey!" Josh counted—and again rushed early, knocking Ben even harder. When Ben kept moaning and couldn't get up from the ground, his dad came running and scooped him into their car and sped to the emergency room.

It took a CAT scan to show Ben's exploded spleen and emergency surgery to save his life. When Josh came to visit Ben at the hospital he saw the tubes sticking into Ben and started to cry. "Your dad told me what the doctors said," Josh finally said. "I'm sorry I did this to you."

"It's okay, Josh," Ben said. "I'm not going to stay mad at you. I forgive you."

☞ **Read Psalm 103:8–12. You blew it. You know it. Now what are you supposed to do?**

You can't unrupture a spleen you bounced to shreds. Or reel nasty words back into your mouth. Or uncheat on a test. Nothing can completely undo what you did—whether it's a sin or a mistake or a bit of both. But you *can* do *what you can* to make things right: Say you're sorry. Talk nicer next time. Turn yourself in to the teacher and take a zero or retake the test.

But squashing people is only half our problem when we do wrong. So setting that straight is only half our job. Our sin also snubs God. "You are not a God who takes pleasure in evil; with you the wicked cannot dwell," David wrote. "The arrogant cannot stand in your presence; you hate all who do wrong" (Psalm 5:4).

God's anger is bone-crushing stuff. But His forgiveness is even bigger. When you blow it and you know it, tell God. If you admit your sin He wipes it away—completely. He doesn't stay mad.

He's not giving us permission to be bad. He's making us blameless. And offering us a fresh start at following Him.

If we claim to be without sin, we deceive ourselves and the truth is not in us. If we confess our sins, he is faithful and just and will forgive us our sins and purify us from all unrighteousness.

1 JOHN 1:8–9

45

Heading Home

Bekah slouches in her chair, staring at her desk—sure that everyone around her is staring at *her*.

The school play had closed the night before. Bekah went to the cast party with instructions from her parents to be at the front door for her ride home at 10:30—an exceedingly generous school-night curfew, they said. When Bekah didn't come out to the car on time her dad strolled to the front door, rang the doorbell, and bellowed inside. There she was—Bekah Fischer, star of the school play, deserting the party right after it started, exiting hours earlier than anyone else.

In the car she protested to her dad that she wasn't tired at all. But a minute later she zonked. Her dad had to carry her into the house.

Now all that anyone at school cares about is that she—and her dad—pooped all over their party.

That's why they're staring at her.

☑ **Read Hebrews 11:13–16. "These people" in the passage are great believers of the past like Abraham, Joseph, and Moses. How did they feel about their home on planet earth?**

This world has chosen to run from God. So if you're trying to run *toward* Him you're going to bang heads with people going the other way. Big things, little things—you'll clash with your classmates. You won't always fit perfectly with your peers.

The problem isn't your parents—they just want what's best for you. It isn't God—what He commands is always good. It isn't you—provided you're trying to do what's right. It isn't even the people around you. It's bigger than that.

The real problem is that this planet isn't your home. As a Christian you're a citizen of heaven (Philippians 3:20). And that makes you an "alien" and "stranger" here.

When we follow God we always ache for something better. But it isn't until heaven that we receive *all* that God has promised: A room in God's mansion (John 14:2). A spot in the city of God, where there's no more crying or pain (Revelation 21:3–4). A forever family where no one will argue about what's wrong and right (Hebrews 8:11).

It's where we belong.

It's a long walk before we get there.

But it's the one place where we'll feel totally at home.

They did not receive the things promised; they only saw them and welcomed them from a distance. And they admitted that they were aliens and strangers on earth. . . . They were longing for a better country—a heavenly one.

HEBREWS 11:13B, 16

Acknowledgments

Thanks first and foremost to our parents—Roy and Lois Johnson and Tom and Pat Benson—and to their parents and their parents' parents. We know how incredibly fortunate we are to come from families who for generations have known and followed God.

Thank you to everyone at Bethany House Publishers, for being great friends, coworkers, and bosses.

And thanks to my family—to Lyn for loving me, keeping me sane, and being my partner in raising Nate, Karin, and Elise. And to you three great kids for making life too much fun.

Kevin Walter Johnson